C000152742

contents

NZ, Canada, US and UK readers
Please note that Australian cup and
spoon measurements are metric.
A conversion chart appears on page 62.

handy hints for scrumptious

Following these useful tips will ensure that every recipe in this book

Trifles

- Trifles are best made a day ahead of serving; decorate them on the day of serving.
- Partially set jelly should be the consistency of egg white.
- Cool custard with plastic wrap or damp baking paper placed directly onto the surface of the custard – this will prevent a skin forming.
- Most trifle recipes can be adapted to use either fresh or canned fruit.

Pavlovas

- Cooks and scientists argue about the ideal temperature of egg whites used to make meringue. Some say they are best beaten at room temperature; others advocate beating egg whites at refrigerator temperature. We found eggs at both temperatures could be beaten to a good volume.
- When separating the egg whites from the yolks, be careful not to include even the smallest amount of yolk with the white – the fat content in

yolk will prevent egg whites from foaming. Always break each egg separately into a cup before adding to the bowl for beating.
- Use a small deep bowl to beat egg whites – this ensures the beaters are well into the whites and will build up the greatest volume.
- Make sure the bowl is dry and clean – any greasy residue in the bowl will prevent egg whites from beating up.
- Beat egg whites on highest speed of the electric mixer until thick and white, but not dry. When they look glossy and have firm, soft peaks, add sugar. If egg whites are beaten until they are dry, it is more difficult to dissolve the sugar.
- Use caster sugar in pavlovas as it will dissolve faster than granulated sugar.
- Add 1 tablespoon of sugar to beaten egg whites at a time; let it dissolve before adding the next spoonful.
- Sugar grains can be felt by rubbing a small amount of meringue mixture between fingers.

desserts

results in dessert perfection!

- Make sure that there are no sugar grains around the top of the beaters or around the sides of the bowl; scrape the mixture down the bowl with a spatula. Keep beating on high speed while adding the sugar.
- Total beating time should be about 10 minutes, to ensure every grain of sugar is completely dissolved.
- To prepare oven trays: brush tray lightly but evenly with melted butter, sprinkle evenly with cornflour or plain flour then shake off excess flour. Alternatively you can line an oven tray with aluminum foil or baking paper; there is no need to grease the foil or baking paper.
- Cool meringue in the oven with the door ajar; if meringue is cooled too quickly it can crack.
- Don't worry if your pavlova cracks in a few spots; you can simply cover the cracks with cream.
- Store unfilled pavlova in an airtight container; fill and decorate pavlova about an hour before serving.

Cheesecakes

- Every brand of springform tin gives a different measurement; the measurement we have used is the width across the inside-top of the tin, when the tin is closed.
- Use plain, sweet, un-iced biscuits to make the crumbs.
- For easy removal of cheesecake from its tin, cover the base of the springform tin with foil.
- If a crumb mixture is lining the base and side of springform tin, it's not necessary to grease the tin. If, however, a crumb mixture is only on the base of the tin, you should grease the side of the tin.
- If large cracks appear on the surface of the cheesecake after cooking, it could be due to: over-cooking; the oven temperature being too high; over- beating the mixture; or the cheesecake having been cooled too quickly (it should always be cooled in the oven, with the door ajar).

baked banana cheesecake

1½ cups (225g)
   plain flour
¼ cup (40g) icing
   sugar mixture
90g butter
2 egg yolks
1 tablespoon cold water,
   approximately
2 x 250g packets cream
   cheese, softened
½ cup (110g)
   caster sugar
2 teaspoons vanilla
   essence
1½ cups mashed
   banana
3 eggs, beaten lightly

You need about 3 large overripe bananas (700g)
for this recipe.

Sift flour and icing sugar into medium bowl,
rub in butter; add egg yolks and enough of
the water to make ingredients cling together.
Press mixture into a ball; knead on floured surface
until smooth. Cover; refrigerate 30 minutes.

Press pastry evenly over base and side of
23cm springform tin, trim edge, lightly prick base
with fork. Cover; refrigerate 30 minutes.

Preheat oven to moderately hot. Cover pastry
with baking paper, fill with dried beans or rice.
Bake in moderately hot oven 10 minutes; remove
paper and beans. Bake 15 minutes or until
browned lightly; cool.

Meanwhile, reduce oven temperature to
moderate. Beat cheese, sugar and essence in
medium bowl with electric mixer until smooth;
add banana and egg, beat until smooth.

Place tin on oven tray, pour cheesecake mixture
into tin. Bake in moderate oven about 1¼ hours
or until just firm. Cool in oven with door ajar.
Cover, refrigerate 3 hours or overnight.

serves 10
per serving 26.4g fat; 1777kJ (425 cal)

lemon curd cheesecake

250g plain sweet biscuits
125g butter, melted
3 x 250g packets cream cheese, softened
½ cup (110g) caster sugar
2 teaspoons finely grated lemon rind
3 eggs
lemon curd
45g butter
½ cup (110g) caster sugar
1 egg, beaten lightly, strained
1 teaspoon finely grated lemon rind
2 tablespoons lemon juice

Process biscuits until mixture resembles fine breadcrumbs.
Add butter; process until just combined.
Using one hand, press crumb mixture evenly over base
and side of 21cm springform tin. Cover; refrigerate
30 minutes or until firm.
Meanwhile, preheat oven to moderate. Beat cheese,
sugar and rind in large bowl with electric mixer until smooth;
beat in eggs, one at a time.
Place tin on oven tray, pour cheesecake mixture into tin.
Bake in moderate oven about 1 hour or until set. Remove
from oven; cool in tin to room temperature.
Spread top of cheesecake with lemon curd; refrigerate
3 hours or overnight. Remove from tin just before serving.
Lemon curd Combine ingredients in medium heatproof
bowl. Place bowl over medium saucepan of simmering water;
cook, stirring constantly, about 20 minutes or until mixture
coats the back of a spoon. Remove bowl from saucepan
immediately to avoid further cooking; cool to room temperature.

serves 10
per serving 45.1g fat; 2541kJ (607 cal)

caramel crunch cheesecake

125g plain chocolate
  biscuits
60g butter, melted
2 x 250g packets cream
  cheese, softened
⅓ cup (75g) caster sugar
2 teaspoons grated
  lemon rind
3 eggs
⅓ cup (80ml) cream
1 tablespoon plain flour
50g bar chocolate-
  coated honeycomb,
  chopped finely
caramel filling
30g butter
¼ cup (50g) firmly packed
  brown sugar
2 tablespoons sweetened
  condensed milk
1 tablespoon golden syrup
2 tablespoons hot water
chocolate topping
150g dark eating
  chocolate, chopped
¼ cup (60ml) cream

Line base of 21cm springform tin with foil,
line side with baking paper.

Process biscuits until mixture resembles
fine breadcrumbs. Add butter; process until
just combined.

Using one hand, press crumb mixture evenly
over base of prepared tin. Cover; refrigerate
30 minutes or until firm.

Meanwhile, preheat oven to slow. Beat
cheese, sugar and rind in medium bowl with
electric mixer until smooth; beat in eggs,
one at a time. Add cream and flour; beat until
smooth. Stir honeycomb and the caramel filling
into cheese mixture.

Place tin on oven tray, pour cheesecake mixture
into tin. Bake in slow oven about 1¼ hours or
until just firm. Cool in oven with door ajar.

Spread the chocolate topping over cheesecake.
Cover cheesecake; refrigerate 3 hours or
overnight. Remove from tin just before serving.

Caramel filling Combine ingredients in
small saucepan; stir over low heat until sugar
is dissolved. Boil, stirring occasionally, about
4 minutes or until a deep caramel colour; cool.

Chocolate topping Combine chocolate
and cream in small saucepan, stir over low
heat until chocolate has melted and mixture
is smooth; cool.

serves 8
per serving 48g fat; 2792kJ (668 cal)

plum and orange baked cheesecake

150g plain sweet
  biscuits
80g butter, melted
825g can dark plums
  in syrup
2 x 250g packets cream
  cheese, softened
2 tablespoons plain
  flour, sifted
½ cup (120g) sour cream
1 teaspoon grated
  orange rind
1 tablespoon
  Grand Marnier
3 eggs, beaten lightly
¾ cup (165g)
  caster sugar
2 tablespoons
  flaked almonds
plum syrup
¼ cup (60ml)
  Grand Marnier
2 teaspoons shredded
  orange rind

Grease side of 23cm springform tin.

Process biscuits until mixture resembles fine breadcrumbs. Add butter; process until just combined.

Using one hand, press crumb mixture evenly over base of prepared tin. Cover; refrigerate 30 minutes or until firm.

Meanwhile, preheat oven to slow. Drain plums over a jug; reserve juice for the plum syrup. Halve plums and remove the stones.

Combine remaining ingredients, except the almonds, in a large bowl. Beat with electric mixer for about 5 minutes or until thick and smooth.

Place tin on oven tray, pour cheesecake mixture into tin, top with plums and sprinkle with almonds. Bake in slow oven about 50 minutes, or until just firm. Cool in oven with door ajar.

Cover cheesecake; refrigerate 3 hours or overnight. Remove from tin just before serving. Serve cheesecake with plum syrup.

Plum syrup Place reserved plum juice, liqueur and rind into a medium saucepan, bring to a boil; simmer, uncovered, until reduced by half. Cool.

serves 8
per serving 41g fat; 2763kJ (661 cal)

tip Orange juice can be substituted for Grand Marnier in the plum syrup, if desired.

baked vanilla cheesecake with poached pears and apricots

250g plain sweet biscuits
125g butter, melted
3 x 250g packets cream
   cheese, softened
¾ cup (165g) caster sugar
2 tablespoons
   vanilla essence
½ teaspoon grated
   lemon rind
2 tablespoons lemon juice
4 eggs, separated
¾ cup (180ml) cream
poached pears
   and apricots
2 cups (500ml) water
1 cup (250ml) orange juice
¼ cup (55g) sugar
1 cup (150g) dried apricots
5 small pears (900g),
   peeled, halved, cored
1 cinnamon stick
¼ teaspoon ground
   nutmeg
2 tablespoons Cointreau

Process biscuits until mixture resembles fine breadcrumbs. Add butter; process until just combined.

Using one hand, press crumb mixture evenly over base and side of 23cm springform tin. Cover; refrigerate 30 minutes or until firm.

Meanwhile, preheat oven to moderately slow. Beat cheese, sugar and essence in large bowl with electric mixer until smooth. Add rind, juice, egg yolks and cream, beat until light and fluffy. Beat two of the egg whites in small bowl with electric mixer until firm peaks form, fold into cream cheese mixture; discard remaining egg whites.

Place tin on oven tray, pour cheesecake mixture into tin. Bake in moderately slow oven about 1 hour or until just firm. Cool in oven with door ajar.

Cover cheesecake; refrigerate 3 hours or overnight. Remove from tin just before serving. Serve cheesecake with poached pears and apricots.

Poached pears and apricots Combine ingredients in large saucepan; simmer, covered, about 10 minutes or until pears are just tender; discard cinnamon stick. Strain fruit mixture over large heatproof bowl, return liquid to same pan; boil, uncovered, about 10 minutes or until reduced to 1 cup (250ml). Add syrup to fruit in bowl.

serves 10
per serving 48.1g fat; 3016kJ (721 cal)

mars bar cheesecake

250g plain chocolate
   biscuits
150g butter, melted
2 tablespoons
   brown sugar
20g butter, extra
300ml thickened cream
50g milk chocolate,
   chopped finely
3 teaspoons gelatine
¼ cup (60ml) water
2 x 250g packets cream
   cheese, softened
½ cup (110g) caster sugar
3 x 60g Mars bars,
   chopped finely

Process biscuits until mixture resembles fine breadcrumbs. Add butter; process until just combined. Using one hand, press crumb mixture evenly over base and side of 21cm springform tin. Cover; refrigerate 30 minutes or until firm.

Meanwhile, combine brown sugar, extra butter and 2 tablespoons of the cream in small saucepan; stir over low heat, until sugar dissolves, to make butterscotch sauce.

Combine chocolate and another 2 tablespoons of the cream in another small saucepan; stir over low heat until chocolate melts.

Sprinkle gelatine over the water in small heatproof jug; stand jug in small saucepan of simmering water. Stir until gelatine dissolves; cool 5 minutes.

Beat cheese and caster sugar in medium bowl with electric mixer until smooth. Beat remaining cream in small bowl with electric mixer until soft peaks form. Stir slightly warm gelatine mixture into cheese mixture with Mars bars; fold in cream.

Pour half of the cheese mixture into prepared tin; drizzle half of the butterscotch and chocolate sauces over cheese mixture. Pull skewer backwards and forward through mixture several times to create marbled effect. Repeat process with remaining cheese mixture and sauces. Cover cheesecake; refrigerate 3 hours or until set.

serves 8
per serving 62.9g fat; 3477kJ (832 cal)

tip You can also melt the milk chocolate and cream in a microwave oven; cook on HIGH (100%) about 1 minute, stirring twice during cooking time.

sticky date cheesecake

This cheesecake can be served warm or at room temperature.

1 cup (170g) dried dates, pitted, chopped
¾ cup (180ml) water
3 x 250g packets cream cheese, softened
2 eggs, beaten lightly
⅔ cup (150g) firmly packed brown sugar
¼ teaspoon ground cinnamon
¼ teaspoon mixed spice
½ cup (40g) flaked almonds
1 teaspoon cinnamon sugar
⅔ cup (150g) firmly packed brown sugar, extra
½ cup (125ml) cream
100g butter, chopped

Grease 23cm springform tin; line base and side
with baking paper.
Combine dates and the water in medium saucepan;
simmer, uncovered, 5 minutes. Strain dates over medium
saucepan; reserve liquid, cool dates.
Meanwhile, preheat oven to moderately slow. Beat
cheese in large bowl with electric mixer until smooth; add
egg, sugar and spices; beat until combined, fold in dates.
Place tin on oven tray, pour cheesecake mixture into tin.
Sprinkle with almonds and cinnamon sugar. Bake in
moderately slow oven about 1 hour, or until firm. Cool
in oven with door ajar.
Stir remaining ingredients into reserved date liquid
in pan, stir over heat until butter is melted; simmer,
uncovered, 2 minutes.
Serve cheesecake with warm sauce.

serves 10
per serving 41.2g fat; 2366kJ (566 cal)

light blackberry cheesecake

2 cups (200g) frozen blackberries
200g low-fat cottage cheese
250g light spreadable cream cheese
2 teaspoons vanilla essence
¾ cup (165g) caster sugar
2 eggs
⅓ cup (55g) semolina
¼ cup (35g) self-raising flour
¼ cup (60ml) buttermilk

Place blackberries in a single layer on absorbent paper; stand at room temperature until thawed.
Preheat oven to moderately slow. Grease 21cm springform tin; line base with baking paper.
Beat cheeses, essence and sugar in large bowl with electric mixer until smooth. Add eggs, one at a time, beating until combined. Stir in semolina and sifted flour, then buttermilk.
Place tin on oven tray. Pour cheesecake mixture into prepared tin. Top with blackberries.
Bake in moderately slow oven about 45 minutes or until just firm. Cool in tin.
Serve dusted with sifted icing sugar, if desired.

serves 8
per serving 7.2g fat; 966kJ (231 cal)

raspberry white chocolate cheesecake

200g plain chocolate
  biscuits
½ cup (90g) finely
  chopped white
  chocolate
80g butter, melted
½ cup (125ml) cream
200g white chocolate,
  extra, chopped
1 cup (250g)
  mascarpone cheese
250g packet
  cream cheese
½ cup (110g)
  caster sugar
3 eggs
2 egg whites
400g fresh raspberries

Process biscuits until mixture resembles fine breadcrumbs. Add chocolate and butter; process until just combined.

Using one hand, press crumb mixture evenly over base and side of 25cm springform tin. Cover; refrigerate 30 minutes or until firm.

Meanwhile, preheat oven to slow. Place cream in small saucepan, bring just to a boil, pour over extra chocolate in small bowl; stir until melted, cool slightly. Beat cheeses and sugar in medium bowl with electric mixer until smooth; beat in eggs, one at a time, then chocolate mixture, beating until just combined. Beat egg whites in clean small bowl with electric mixer until soft peaks form, fold into chocolate mixture with 250g of the raspberries.

Place tin on oven tray, pour cheesecake mixture into tin. Bake in slow oven about 1½ hours or until just firm. Cool in oven with door ajar.

Cover cheesecake; refrigerate 3 hours or overnight. Remove from tin just before serving. Top cheesecake with remaining raspberries and dust with sifted icing sugar, if desired.

serves 10
per serving 42.5g fat; 2478kJ (593 cal)

ripe cherry cheesecake

125g plain chocolate
 biscuits
75g butter, melted
2 x 250g packets cream
 cheese, softened
⅓ cup (75g) caster sugar
2 eggs
200g dark eating
 chocolate, melted
2 x 85g Cherry Ripe
 chocolate bars,
 chopped coarsely
425g can seeded
 black cherries
 in syrup, drained

Grease side of 25cm springform tin.
Process biscuits until mixture resembles
fine breadcrumbs. Add butter; process until
just combined. Using one hand, press crumb
mixture evenly over base of prepared tin. Cover;
refrigerate 30 minutes or until firm.
Preheat oven to moderate.
Meanwhile, beat cheese and sugar in medium
bowl with electric mixer until smooth; add eggs,
one at a time, beating well between additions.
Gradually beat in chocolate; fold Cherry Ripe
and cherries into cheesecake mixture.
Place tin on oven tray. Spread cheesecake
mixture into tin; bake in moderate oven about
50 minutes or until set. Cool in oven with door ajar.
Cover; refrigerate 3 hours or overnight.
Serve cheesecake decorated with chocolate
roses, if desired.

serves 10
per serving 35.6g fat; 2111kJ (505 cal)

tips Use absorbent paper to soak up liquid
from the cherries.
Chocolate should be cool, but not set, before it
is added to the cheesecake mixture.
To make chocolate roses, melt your choice of
chocolate then spread evenly over marble or
foil-covered surface. When chocolate is almost set,
drag ice-cream scoop over surface of chocolate
to make roses.

apricot nectar cheesecake

155g plain sweet
  biscuits
75g butter, melted
2 cups (500ml)
  apricot nectar
1 tablespoon gelatine
375g cream cheese,
  softened
½ cup (110g)
  caster sugar
1 tablespoon lemon juice
1 cup (250ml) cream
topping
1 tablespoon sugar
3 teaspoons cornflour

Line side of 21cm springform tin with baking paper.

Process biscuits until mixture resembles fine breadcrumbs. Add butter; process until just combined.

Using one hand, press crumb mixture evenly over base of tin. Cover; refrigerate 30 minutes or until firm.

Meanwhile, pour 1 cup of the apricot nectar into small saucepan; reserve remaining apricot nectar for the topping. Sprinkle gelatine over nectar in saucepan, place over low heat and stir until gelatine dissolves; cool until thickened slightly. Beat cream cheese and sugar in small bowl with electric mixer until smooth, add lemon juice. Beat in apricot mixture, then fold in whipped cream.

Pour cheesecake mixture into tin; refrigerate 3 hours. Pour topping over cheesecake, refrigerate overnight.

Topping Combine sugar and cornflour in small saucepan; gradually stir in reserved apricot nectar. Bring mixture to a boil, stirring constantly, until mixture boils and thickens slightly; cool.

serves 8
per serving 37.8g fat; 2203kJ (527 cal)

black forest cheesecake

250g plain chocolate
  biscuits
125g butter, melted
250g packet cream
  cheese, softened
¾ cup (165g)
  caster sugar
1 tablespoon lemon juice
3 teaspoons gelatine
½ cup (125ml) water
300ml thickened cream
425g can pitted
  black cherries
topping
1 tablespoon cornflour
1 tablespoon
  caster sugar
1 tablespoon dark rum

Process biscuits until mixture resembles fine breadcrumbs. Add butter; process until just combined.

Using one hand, press crumb mixture evenly over base and side of 21cm springform tin. Cover; refrigerate 30 minutes or until firm.

Meanwhile, beat cheese, sugar and juice in small bowl with electric mixer until smooth and creamy; transfer to large bowl. Sprinkle gelatine over the water in small heatproof jug; stand jug in small saucepan of simmering water. Stir until gelatine dissolves; cool 5 minutes. Whip cream until soft peaks form, fold into cheese mixture; fold in gelatine mixture.

Drain cherries, reserve ¾ cup syrup for topping.

Spoon one-third of cheesecake mixture into tin, top with half of the cherries, then continue layering, ending with cheese mixture; refrigerate 3 hours or overnight until set.

Spread topping over cheesecake, swirl gently into cheese mixture. Refrigerate until set.

Topping Blend cornflour and sugar with reserved cherry syrup in small saucepan. Stir over heat until mixture boils and thickens, stir in rum; cool 10 minutes before using.

serves 8
per serving 42.6g fat; 2512kJ (601 cal)

sicilian cheesecake

185g plain chocolate biscuits
90g butter, melted
½ cup (125ml) cream, whipped
60g dark eating chocolate, grated coarsely
filling
650g ricotta cheese
1 cup (160g) icing sugar
1 teaspoon vanilla essence
2 tablespoons crème de cacao
2 tablespoons finely chopped mixed peel
60g dark eating chocolate, grated finely

Process biscuits until mixture resembles
fine breadcrumbs. Add butter; process until
just combined.
Using one hand, press crumb mixture evenly
over base of greased 21cm springform tin.
Cover; refrigerate 30 minutes or until firm.
Spoon filling over biscuit base; refrigerate
at least 6 hours or overnight.
Serve cream spooned onto wedges of cake.
Sprinkle with chocolate.
Filling Beat cheese, sugar, essence and
crème de cacao in large bowl with electric
mixer until smooth and fluffy. Add peel and
chocolate; mix well.

serves 10
per serving 26.4g fat; 1792kJ (428 cal)

classic refrigerator cheesecake

250g plain sweet biscuits
125g butter, melted
250g packet cream cheese, softened
400g can sweetened condensed milk
2 teaspoons grated lemon rind
⅓ cup (80ml) lemon juice
1 teaspoon gelatine
1 tablespoon water

Process biscuits until mixture resembles fine breadcrumbs. Add butter; process until just combined.

Using one hand, press crumb mixture evenly over base and side of 21cm springform tin. Cover; refrigerate 30 minutes or until firm.

Meanwhile, beat cheese in small bowl with electric mixer until smooth, beat in condensed milk, rind and juice; beat until smooth. Sprinkle gelatine over the water in small heatproof jug; stand jug in small saucepan of simmering water. Stir until gelatine dissolves; cool 5 minutes. Stir gelatine mixture into cheese mixture.

Pour cheesecake mixture into tin; refrigerate 3 hours or overnight until set. Serve with whipped cream, if desired.

serves 8
per serving 32.9g fat; 2207kJ (528 cal)

marshmallow pavlova

4 egg whites
1 cup (220g) caster sugar
1 tablespoon cornflour
1 teaspoon white vinegar
300ml thickened cream
2 teaspoons vanilla essence
1 tablespoon icing sugar
1 passionfruit
150g blueberries

Preheat oven to very slow. Mark an 18cm circle
on baking paper; place paper, marking-side down,
on greased oven tray.
Beat egg whites in small bowl with electric
mixer until soft peaks form; gradually add sugar,
beating until dissolved after additions. Fold in
cornflour and vinegar.
Spread meringue inside circle on prepared tray.
For best results, do not squash or flatten mixture,
but shape side up and in towards centre, like a
mound. Make furrows up side of meringue using
small spatula; level top.
Bake in very slow oven about 1¼ hours or until dry.
Turn oven off; leave meringue to cool in oven with
door ajar. An hour before serving, beat cream,
essence and icing sugar until soft peaks form.
Top meringue with cream mixture; decorate
with passionfruit and berries. Lightly dust with
extra sifted icing sugar, if desired.

serves 6
per serving 18.4g fat; 1464kJ (350 cal)

classic pavlova

4 egg whites
1 cup (220g) caster sugar
300ml thickened cream, whipped
3 cups chopped mixed fresh fruit

Preheat oven to very slow. Cover a greased
oven tray with a piece of baking paper.
Place egg whites in small clean dry bowl; using an
electric mixer, beat on high speed about 1 minute
or until soft peaks form. Gradually add sugar,
about 1 tablespoon at a time, beating well after
each addition, until sugar dissolves.
Spoon meringue into a round shape, approximately
20cm in diameter, on prepared oven tray; level
top of meringue with rubber spatula.
Bake, uncovered, in very slow oven about
1½ hours or until meringue feels firm and dry to
the touch. Turn oven off; open oven door and leave
ajar to cool meringue slowly in oven.
Turn meringue onto serving platter so base
faces upwards; top with cream and fruit.

serves 6
per serving 19g fat; 1482kJ (355 cal)

tip The fruit used to top a pavlova is dependent on
seasonal availability, although the classic pavlova is
usually topped with mixed berries and passionfruit
pulp. Our version uses carambola, nectarine,
green apple, strawberries and raspberries.

pavlova roll

You will need two passionfruit for this recipe.

4 egg whites
½ cup (110g) caster sugar
2 tablespoons caster sugar, extra
2 cups (500ml) thickened cream, whipped
250g strawberries, halved
1 medium kiwi fruit (85g), sliced
2 tablespoons passionfruit pulp

Preheat oven to moderately hot. Grease 26cm x 32cm
swiss roll pan, line base with baking paper, extending
paper 5cm over edges of long sides of pan.
Beat egg whites in small bowl with electric mixer
until soft peaks form; add sugar, in batches,
beating until dissolved between additions.
Spread the mixture into prepared pan.
Bake in moderately hot oven about 10 minutes
or until lightly browned. Turn meringue onto sheet
of baking paper sprinkled with extra sugar.
Gently peel away and discard lining paper;
stand meringue 2 minutes.
Spread a third of the whipped cream over slightly
warm meringue. Place strawberries and kiwi fruit
lengthways along centre of meringue; roll meringue
firmly from long side, using paper as a guide. Cover;
refrigerate 30 minutes. Trim ends, cover top of meringue
roll with remaining cream; decorate with passionfruit
pulp. Cover; refrigerate until ready to serve.

serves 6
per serving 30.8g fat; 1714kJ (410 cal)

tip This recipe can be made 3 hours ahead;
store, covered, in refrigerator.

warm pavlovas with berry compote

3 egg whites
2 cups (320g) icing
   sugar mixture
½ cup (125ml)
   boiling water
300ml thickened
   cream, whipped
berry compote
½ cup (125ml) raspberry
   cranberry fruit drink
1 tablespoon lemon juice
¼ cup (55g) caster sugar
1 tablespoon cornflour
1 tablespoon water
500g frozen
   mixed berries

Place oven rack on lowest shelf. Preheat oven to moderate. Line large oven tray with baking paper.
Beat egg whites, icing sugar and the water in small bowl with electric mixer about 8 minutes or until firm peaks form.
Using a large metal spoon, drop six equal portions of mixture onto prepared tray. Bake on the lowest shelf in moderate oven about 25 minutes or until pavlovas are firm to touch.
Serve pavlovas immediately, topped with warm berry compote and whipped cream.
Berry compote Combine fruit drink, juice and sugar in medium saucepan; stir over heat, without boiling, until sugar is completely dissolved. Blend cornflour and water to a smooth paste, add to saucepan; stir over heat until mixture boils and thickens. Stir in mixed berries.

serves 6
per serving 18.9g fat; 1981kJ (474 cal)

tip Berry compote can be made a day ahead and served cold, or reheated to serve warm with pavlovas. Pavlovas must be made close to serving as they will deflate.

coffee hazelnut meringues

3 egg whites
½ cup (110g) caster sugar
1 teaspoon ground coffee (not instant)
½ cup (60g) chopped toasted hazelnuts
¾ cup (180ml) thickened cream
2 tablespoons Kahlúa
75g dark eating chocolate, melted

Preheat oven to slow. Beat egg whites in small bowl with electric mixer until soft peaks form; gradually add caster sugar, beating until dissolved after each addition. Fold in coffee.

Using a large metal spoon, drop four equal portions of mixture onto baking-paper-lined oven tray; sprinkle pavlovas with half of the nuts.

Bake in slow oven about 1 hour or until pavlovas are dry and crisp. Cool in oven with door ajar.

Beat cream and liqueur in small bowl with electric mixer until soft peaks form.

Just before serving, top meringues with whipped cream mixture; drizzle with melted chocolate and sprinkle with remaining nuts.

serves 4
per serving 31.2g fat; 2103kJ (503 cal)

tip To remove the skin from hazelnuts, place nuts on oven tray and bake in moderate oven about 10 minutes or until skins start to split. Rub warmed nuts together with a tea towel to remove skin.

tropical fruit mini pavlovas

6 egg whites
1½ cups (330g) caster sugar
300ml thickened cream, whipped
1 medium kiwi fruit (85g), peeled, halved, sliced thinly
1 small mango (100g), peeled, sliced thinly
2 passionfruit
shaved fresh or flaked dry coconut, optional

Preheat oven to very slow. Draw eight 8.5cm circles
on a large sheet of baking paper. Grease an oven
tray; place paper, marking-side down, on tray.
Beat egg whites in large bowl with electric mixer
until soft peaks form, gradually add sugar, continue
beating until sugar is dissolved (about 10 minutes).
Divide mixture evenly among circles, shape using
a palate knife. Bake in very slow oven about
30 minutes or until crisp and dry. Cool pavlovas
in oven with door ajar.
Just before serving, top pavlovas with whipped
cream, fruit and coconut, if desired.

serves 8
per serving 13.9g fat; 1308kJ (313 cal)

classic trifle

85g packet raspberry
 jelly crystals
250g sponge cake
2 tablespoons
 raspberry jam
¼ cup (60ml)
 sweet sherry
¼ cup (30g)
 custard powder
¼ cup (55g) caster sugar
1½ cups (375ml) milk
825g can sliced
 peaches, drained
1½ cups (375ml)
 thickened cream
1 teaspoon
 vanilla essence
2 tablespoons flaked
 almonds, toasted

Make jelly according to directions on packet;
pour into a shallow container (such as a cake pan).
Cover and refrigerate 20 minutes or until jelly
is almost set.
Meanwhile, split cake in half, spread bottom
half of the cake with jam; replace top. Cut into
3cm pieces.
Arrange cake pieces in a 3.5-litre (14 cup)
serving dish; sprinkle with sherry.
Combine custard powder, sugar and 1 tablespoon
of the milk in small saucepan; stir in remaining milk.
Stir over heat until mixture boils and thickens.
Cover surface with damp baking paper or
cling wrap to prevent a skin forming; cool.
Pour almost-set jelly over cake, cover;
refrigerate 15 minutes or until jelly is set.
Arrange the peach slices over the jelly.
Stir ½ cup (125ml) of the cream and vanilla
into custard; pour over peaches.
Whip remaining cream; spread over custard,
sprinkle with flaked almonds. Refrigerate
several hours or overnight.

serves 8
per serving 21.5g fat; 1859kJ (445 cal)

raspberry and chocolate mousse trifle

150g dark eating
  chocolate,
  chopped coarsely
½ cup (125ml)
  thickened cream
1 egg, separated
2 teaspoons caster sugar
85g packet raspberry
  jelly crystals
200g packaged chocolate
  savoiardi sponge-finger
  biscuits (approximately 6)
¼ cup (60ml) coffee-
  flavoured liqueur
1 cup (135g) raspberries
300ml thickened
  cream, extra

Tia Maria and Kahlúa are two coffee-flavoured liqueurs; either of them can be used in this recipe.

Combine chocolate and cream in small saucepan; stir over heat, without boiling, until smooth. Remove from heat; whisk in egg yolk. Transfer to medium bowl.
Place egg white and sugar in small bowl; beat with electric mixer until sugar dissolves. Gently fold egg white mixture into chocolate mixture. Cover; refrigerate mousse 3 hours or overnight.
Meanwhile, make jelly according to directions on packet; pour into a shallow container (such as a cake pan). Cover and refrigerate 20 minutes or until jelly is almost set.
Cut sponge fingers into 1.5cm slices. Place slices over base and around side of deep 2-litre (8 cup) serving bowl; drizzle evenly with liqueur. Pour almost-set jelly over sponge fingers; refrigerate until jelly sets.
Sprinkle half of the raspberries over jelly; spread evenly with mousse. Top with whipped extra cream and remaining raspberries. Sprinkle with chocolate shavings, if desired.

serves 6
per serving 36.9g fat; 2541kJ (608 cal)

tips Mousse can be prepared up to two days ahead; trifle can be assembled one day ahead. If fresh raspberries are not available, substitute frozen raspberries that have been thawed.

tropical trifle

3 eggs, separated
½ cup (110g) caster sugar
¾ cup (105g) self-
   raising flour
2 tablespoons hot milk
2 tablespoons caster
   sugar, extra
¾ cup (240g) lemon butter
2 x 85g packets
   lemon jelly crystals
½ cup (125ml)
   sweet sherry
300ml thickened
   cream, whipped
1 medium mango (430g),
   peeled, sliced
2 medium kiwi fruit (170g),
   peeled, sliced
2 passionfruit
custard
¾ cup (120g)
   custard powder
1 cup (220g) sugar
3 cups (750ml) milk
300ml thickened cream
2 teaspoons
   vanilla essence
4 egg yolks

Preheat oven to hot. Grease 25cm x 30cm swiss roll pan; line base and sides with baking paper.

Beat egg whites in small bowl with electric mixer until soft peaks form; gradually beat in sugar, beat until dissolved. Beat in egg yolks, transfer mixture to large bowl. Gently fold in sifted flour and milk.

Pour mixture into prepared pan. Bake in hot oven 8 minutes or until sponge is elastic to touch and lightly browned. Turn quickly onto baking paper sprinkled with extra sugar, peel off lining paper. Cut off crisp edges from long sides. Spread sponge evenly with lemon butter; roll up loosely, from long side, using paper as a guide. Lift roll onto wire rack to cool.

Make jelly according to directions on packet; pour into a shallow container (such as a cake pan). Cover and refrigerate 20 minutes or until jelly is almost set.

Meanwhile, cut swiss roll into slices, place over base of 3.5-litre (14 cup) serving dish. Sprinkle with sherry. Pour almost-set jelly over cake, refrigerate until jelly is set. Pour custard over jelly, refrigerate until cold. Decorate with whipped cream and fruit.

Custard Combine custard powder and sugar in medium saucepan; gradually stir in milk and cream. Stir constantly over heat until mixture boils and thickens. Remove from heat, stir in vanilla and egg yolks, cover surface with damp baking paper or cling wrap to prevent a skin forming; cool to room temperature.

serves 8
per serving 38.1g fat; 3646kJ (872 cal)

tiramisu

2 tablespoons instant coffee powder
1¼ cups (310ml) boiling water
1 cup (250ml) marsala
250g packet savoiardi sponge-finger biscuits
½ cup (125ml) thickened cream
⅓ cup (55g) icing sugar mixture
2 cups (500g) mascarpone cheese
40g dark eating chocolate, grated
125g blueberries

Dissolve coffee in the water in medium bowl. Stir
in ⅔ cup (160ml) of the marsala; cool. Dip half of
the biscuits, one at a time, in coffee mixture; arrange
in single layer in 2.5-litre (10 cup) serving dish.
Beat cream and sifted icing sugar in small bowl
until soft peaks form; transfer to large bowl. Fold
in mascarpone and remaining marsala.
Spread half of the cream mixture over biscuits
in dish. Dip remaining biscuits in remaining
coffee mixture; arrange on top of cream layer.
Top biscuits with remaining cream mixture; sprinkle
with chocolate. Cover, refrigerate several hours or
overnight. Decorate with berries just before serving.

serves 6
per serving 39.2g fat; 3041kJ (726 cal)

tip Tiramisu is best made a day ahead; store,
covered, in the refrigerator.

berry trifle

1¾ cups (430ml) thickened cream
¼ cup (40g) icing sugar mixture
1 teaspoon finely grated orange rind
1 cup (250g) mascarpone
¼ cup (60ml) Cointreau
150g blueberries
250g raspberries
250g strawberries, quartered
1 cup (250ml) fresh orange juice
250g packet savoiardi sponge-finger biscuits

Beat cream, sugar and rind in small bowl with an electric mixer until soft peaks form; fold in mascarpone and 2 teaspoons of the liqueur.
Combine berries and another 2 teaspoons of liqueur in medium bowl.
Combine remaining liqueur and juice in another medium bowl. Dip sponge fingers, one at a time, in juice mixture. Arrange half of the sponge fingers around base of 2-litre (8 cup) serving dish. Top with half of the cream mixture; sprinkle with half of the berry mixture.
Layer remaining sponge fingers over berries. Repeat cream and berry layers. Cover, refrigerate 3 hours or overnight.

serves 6
per serving 42.3g fat; 2621kJ (627 cal)

brandied apricot trifles

2 cups (500ml) milk
¼ cup (30g)
   custard powder
¼ cup (50g) firmly
   packed brown sugar
2 eggs
1 teaspoon vanilla essence
825g can apricots
   in light syrup
1½ cups (375ml)
   apricot nectar
2 tablespoons gelatine
250g packet jam rollettes
⅓ cup (80ml) Cointreau
300ml thickened
   cream, whipped

Jam rollettes are mini swiss rolls.

Bring milk to a boil in medium saucepan, remove from heat. Blend custard powder, sugar and eggs in medium bowl. Beat with electric mixer until sugar is dissolved. Stir egg mixture into milk; stir over heat, without boiling, until custard is slightly thickened. Stir in essence, cover; cool to room temperature.

Drain apricots, reserve syrup. Combine reserved syrup and apricot nectar in medium saucepan, sprinkle with gelatine, stir over heat, without boiling, until gelatine is dissolved; cool to room temperature.

Slice apricots, place into 20cm x 30cm lamington pan. Pour gelatine mixture over apricots; refrigerate until set.

Cut rollettes into 1cm slices, divide half of the slices over bases of six 400ml serving glasses. Sprinkle rollettes with half of the liqueur. Cut apricot jelly into 5cm pieces, arrange half of the jelly over cake, top with half of the custard. Repeat layering with cake, liqueur, jelly and custard. Top with cream.

serves 6
per serving 26.4g fat; 2451kJ (586 cal)

strawberry meringue cream trifle

500g fresh strawberries, quartered
1 tablespoon Grand Marnier
1 cup (250ml) thickened cream
2 tablespoons icing sugar mixture
½ cup (140g) yogurt
10 pavlova nests, chopped coarsely

Combine strawberries and liqueur in medium bowl.
Beat cream and sugar in small bowl with electric
mixer until soft peaks form. Fold in yogurt.
Place half of the strawberry mixture in base
of 1.25-litre (5 cup) serving dish. Top with half
of the meringue and half of the cream mixture.
Repeat the layers.

serves 4
per serving 24.7g fat; 1676kJ (401 cal)

tip If preferred, you can substitute orange juice
for the Grand Marnier.

mango and passionfruit trifle

1 cup (250ml) orange juice
½ cup (125ml) Galliano
250g packet savoiardi
   sponge-finger biscuits
3 medium mangoes
   (1.3kg), sliced
½ cup (125ml)
   passionfruit pulp
½ cup (125ml)
   thickened cream
¼ cup (40g) icing
   sugar mixture
2 cups (500g)
   mascarpone cheese
2 eggs
¼ cup (55g) caster sugar
⅓ cup (55g) vienna
   almonds, chopped
   coarsely

You will need about three large passionfruit for this recipe. Vienna almonds are sugar-coated nuts, available from specialty nut or confectionery stores and some supermarkets.

Combine juice and half of the liqueur in small, shallow bowl. Dip half of the biscuits in juice mixture then place biscuits in single layer over base of 3-litre (12 cup) serving dish.
Top biscuits with half of the mango and passionfruit pulp.
Beat cream and icing sugar in small bowl with electric mixer until firm peaks form. Combine mascarpone and remaining liqueur in large bowl, fold in the cream mixture. Beat eggs and caster sugar in small bowl with electric mixer until thick and creamy. Gently fold the egg mixture into the mascarpone mixture.
Spread half of the mascarpone mixture over the fruit in dish. Dip remaining biscuits in juice mixture and repeat layers with remaining fruit and mascarpone mixture. Cover dish and refrigerate for at least 6 hours.
Sprinkle with vienna almonds.

serves 8
per serving 32g fat; 2495kJ (597 cal)

glossary

almonds flat, pointy-ended
nuts with pitted brown shell
enclosing a creamy white
kernel which is covered by
a brown skin.
  flaked: paper-thin slices
of almond.

brandy spirit distilled from
wine or other fermented
fruit juice.

butter use salted or
unsalted (sweet) butter;
125g is equal to one stick
of butter.

buttermilk sold alongside
all fresh milk products in
supermarkets; despite the
implication of its name,
buttermilk is low in fat.
Originally the liquid left after
cream was separated from
milk; today, it is commercially
made similarly to yogurt.
A good lower-fat substitution
for dairy products such
as cream or sour cream;
good in baking and
salad dressings.

cheese
  cottage: fresh, white,
unripened curd cheese
with a grainy consistency
and a fat content between
5% and 15%.
  cream: commonly known
as Philadelphia or Philly;
a soft cow-milk cheese
with a fat content of at
least 33%. Sold in
supermarkets, in bulk
and packaged. Also
available as spreadable
light cream cheese, a light
version of Philadelphia,
a blend of cottage and
cream cheeses with a fat
content of 21%.

mascarpone: a cultured
cream product made in much
the same way as yogurt. It is
whitish to creamy-yellow in
colour, with a soft, creamy
texture, a fat content of 75%
and a slightly tangy taste.

ricotta: the name for this
soft, white, cow-milk cheese
roughly translates as cooked
again. It's made from whey,
a byproduct of other cheese
making, to which fresh milk
and acid are added. Ricotta is
a sweet, moist cheese with a
fat content of around 8.5%
and a slightly grainy texture

cherry ripe chocolate bar
made from chocolate,
coconut, sugar, cherries,
glucose and milk powder.

chocolate
  dark eating: made of cocoa
liquor, cocoa butter and sugar.
  milk: primarily for eating.
  white: eating chocolate.

cinnamon
  stick: dried inner bark of the
shoots of the cinnamon tree.
  sugar: combination of ground
cinnamon and caster sugar.

cointreau citrus-flavoured
liqueur.

cornflour also known as
cornstarch; used as a
thickening agent in cooking.

cream
  fresh: (minimum fat content
35%) also known as pure
cream and pouring cream;
contains no additives.
  sour: (minimum fat content
35%) a thick, commercially
cultured soured cream.
  thickened: (minimum fat
content 35%) a whipping
cream containing a thickener.

crème de cacao a dark,
chocolate-flavoured liqueur,
with a hint of vanilla.

custard powder instant
mixture used to make pouring
custard; similar to American
instant pudding mixtures.

eggs some recipes in this
book call for raw or barely
cooked eggs; exercise
caution if there is a salmonella
problem in your area.

essences also known as
extracts; usually the byproduct
of distillation of plants.

flour
  plain: an all-purpose flour,
made from wheat.
  self-raising: plain flour sifted
with baking powder in the
proportion of 1 cup flour to
2 teaspoons baking powder.

galliano clear yellow-coloured
Italian liqueur made from
an infusion of various herbs
and flowers.

gelatine we used powdered
gelatine. It is also available
in sheet form, known as
leaf gelatine.

golden syrup a byproduct
of refined sugarcane; pure
maple syrup or honey can
be substituted.

grand marnier orange-
flavoured liqueur based
on Cognac-brandy.

hazelnuts also known as
filberts; plump, grape-size,
rich, sweet nut having a
brown inedible skin that
is removed by rubbing
heated nuts together
vigorously in a tea towel.

jam also known as preserve
or conserve; most often
made from fruit.

jam rollettes also known as sponge rollettes; we used 9cm-long sponge rolls filled with jam or jam and cream; these are generally purchased in 250g packets of six.

jelly crystals available from supermarkets.

kahlúa coffee-flavoured liqueur.

kiwi fruit also known as chinese gooseberry.

lamington pan straight-sided rectangular slab cake pan that is 3cm deep.

lemon butter packaged spread; also known as lemon curd, lemon cheese and lemon spread.

marsala a sweet fortified wine originally from Sicily.

mars bars a chocolate and caramel confectionery bar.

mixed peel candied citrus peel.

mixed spice a blend of ground spices usually consisting of cinnamon, allspice and nutmeg.

nutmeg the dried nut of an evergreen tree native to Indonesia; it is available in ground form or you can grate your own with a fine grater.

pavlova nests available from supermarkets.

rum, dark we prefer to use an underproof rum (not overproof) for a more subtle flavour.

savoiardi also known as savoy biscuits, lady's fingers or sponge fingers, they are Italian-style crisp fingers made from sponge cake mixture.

semolina made from durum wheat milled into various-textured granules, all of which are finer than flour.

sugar we used coarse, granulated table sugar, also known as crystal sugar, unless otherwise specified.

brown: an extremely soft, fine granulated sugar retaining molasses for its characteristic colour and flavour.

caster: also known as superfine or finely granulated table sugar.

icing mixture: also known as confectioners' sugar or powdered sugar; granulated sugar crushed together with a small amount (about 3%) cornflour added.

sweet sherry fortified wine consumed as an aperitif or used in cooking.

sweetened condensed milk milk from which 60% of the water has been removed; the remaining milk is then sweetened with sugar.

vienna almonds toffee-coated almonds.

vinegar, white made from spirit of cane sugar.

yogurt unflavoured, full-fat cow-milk yogurt has been used in these recipes, unless stated otherwise.

conversion chart

MEASURES

One Australian metric measuring cup holds approximately 250ml, one Australian metric tablespoon holds 20ml, one Australian metric teaspoon holds 5ml.

The difference between one country's measuring cups and another's is within a two- or three-teaspoon variance, and will not affect your cooking results. North America, New Zealand and the United Kingdom use a 15ml tablespoon.

All cup and spoon measurements are level. The most accurate way of measuring dry ingredients is to weigh them. When measuring liquids, use a clear glass or plastic jug with the metric markings.

We use large eggs with an average weight of 60g.

DRY MEASURES

METRIC	IMPERIAL
15g	½oz
30g	1oz
60g	2oz
90g	3oz
125g	4oz (¼lb)
155g	5oz
185g	6oz
220g	7oz
250g	8oz (½lb)
280g	9oz
315g	10oz
345g	11oz
375g	12oz (¾lb)
410g	13oz
440g	14oz
470g	15oz
500g	16oz (1lb)
750g	24oz (1½lb)
1kg	32oz (2lb)

LIQUID MEASURES

METRIC	IMPERIAL
30ml	1 fluid oz
60ml	2 fluid oz
100ml	3 fluid oz
125ml	4 fluid oz
150ml	5 fluid oz (¼ pint/1 gill
190ml	6 fluid oz
250ml	8 fluid oz
300ml	10 fluid oz (½ pint)
500ml	16 fluid oz
600ml	20 fluid oz (1 pint)
1000ml (1 litre)	1¾ pints

LENGTH MEASURES

METRIC	IMPERIAL
3mm	⅛in
6mm	¼in
1cm	½in
2cm	¾in
2.5cm	1in
5cm	2in
6cm	2½in
8cm	3in
10cm	4in
13cm	5in
15cm	6in
18cm	7in
20cm	8in
23cm	9in
25cm	10in
28cm	11in
30cm	12in (1ft)

OVEN TEMPERATURES

These oven temperatures are only a guide for conventional ovens. For fan-forced ovens, check the manufacturer's manual.

	°C (CELSIUS)	°F (FAHRENHEIT)	GAS MARK
Very slow	120	250	½
Slow	150	275 – 300	1 – 2
Moderately slow	160	325	3
Moderate	180	350 – 375	4 – 5
Moderately hot	200	400	6
Hot	220	425 – 450	7 – 8
Very hot	240	475	9

index

This book is published by Octopus Publishing Group Limited based on
materials licensed to it by ACP Magazines Ltd, a division of Nine Entertainment Co.
54 Park St, Sydney
GPO Box 4088, Sydney, NSW 2001.
phone (02) 9282 8618; fax (02) 9126 3702
acpbooks@acpmagazines.com.au; www.acpbooks.com.au

ACP BOOKS
Publishing director, ACP Magazines – Gerry Reynolds
Publisher – Sally Wright
Editorial & food director – Pamela Clark
Creative director – Hieu Chi Nguyen
Sales & rights director – Brian Cearnes

Published and Distributed in the United Kingdom by Octopus Publishing Group
Endeavour House
189 Shaftesbury Avenue
London WC2H 8JY
United Kingdom
phone (+44)(0)207 632 5400; fax (+44)(0)207 632 5405
aww@octopus-publishing.co.uk; www.octopusbooks.co.uk
www.australian-womens-weekly.com

Printed and bound in Thailand

Distributed in Canada by Canadian Manda Group
165 Dufferin Street, Toronto
Ontario, Canada M6K 3H6

International foreign language rights, Brian Cearnes, ACP Books bcearnes@acpmagazines.com.au

A catalogue record for this book is available from the British Library.

ISBN 978-1-907428-82-1

Cover Lemon curd cheesecake, page 7.
Stylist – Amber Keller
Photographer – Louise Lister
Additional photography – Ian Wallace
Additional styling – Hieu Chi Nguyen
Food preparation for additional photography – Kelly Cruickshanks

To order Australian Women's Weekly books
telephone LBS on 01903 828 503
or order online at www.octopusbooks.co.uk

Send recipe enquiries to: recipeenquiries@acpmagazines.com.au